WONDERS
OF THE
SEA

Claire Laude and
Aurélie Castex

Color Your Way to Calm

Little, Brown and Company
New York   Boston   London

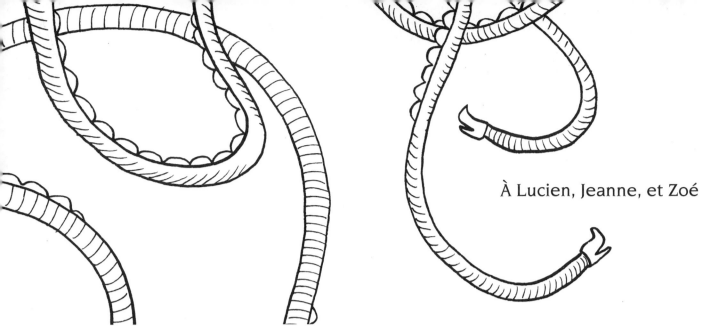

À Lucien, Jeanne, et Zoé

Little, Brown and Company
Hachette Book Group
1290 Avenue of the Americas, New York, NY 10104
littlebrown.com

First North American Edition: December 2015
Originally published as *Merveilles Sous Les Mers* in France by Éditions Marabout, January 2015

Little, Brown and Company is a division of Hachette Book Group, Inc.
The Little, Brown name and logo are trademarks of Hachette Book Group, Inc.

The publisher is not responsible for websites (or their content) that are not owned by the publisher.

The Hachette Speakers Bureau provides a wide range of authors for speaking events. To find out more, go to hachettespeakersbureau.com or call (866) 376-6591.

ISBN 978-0-316-35006-8
Library of Congress Control Number: 2015946920

10 9 8 7 6 5 4 3 2 1

WW

Printed in the United States of America

Arélie Castex and Claire Laude met at the École des Arts Décoratifs in Paris and have been working together since. From their studio in Paris they now weave a wonderful world full of humorous, playful, stylish, and quirky images.

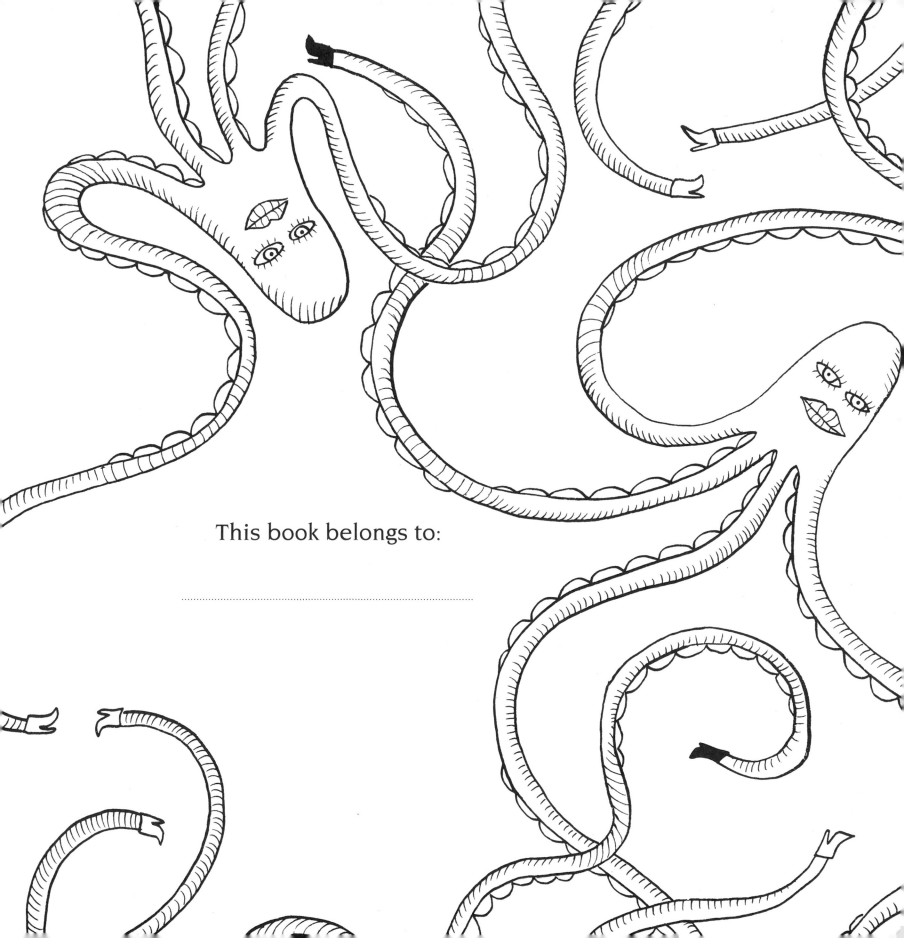

This book belongs to:

....

Dive into our wonderful underwater kingdom!

It's time to leave the surface and dive
down into the depths of the sea.
As you descend, swim through shimmering
mirages and pass by schools of fish, gigantic
whales, playful dolphins, and many other
creatures that are hidden in the aquatic paradise
of this black and white world.

Pick up your pens and pencils to reveal a thousand
underwater secrets. Relax and give your imagination
free rein as you discover the calming and
creative pleasures of coloring in.

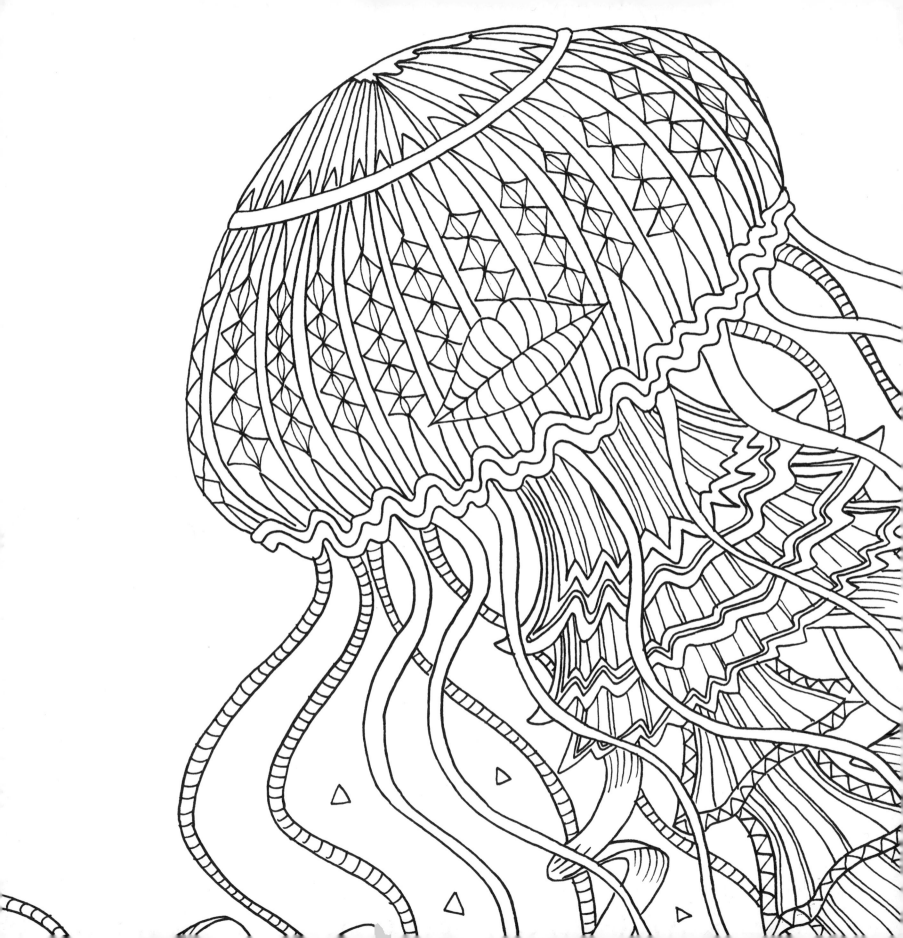

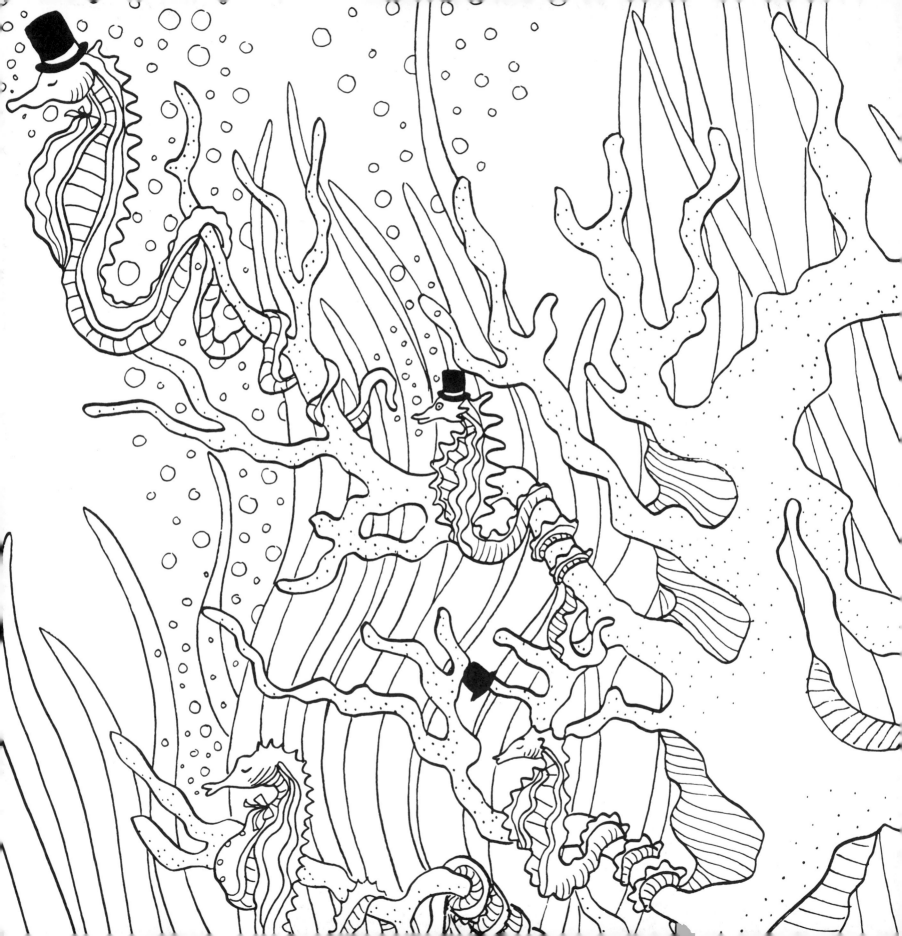

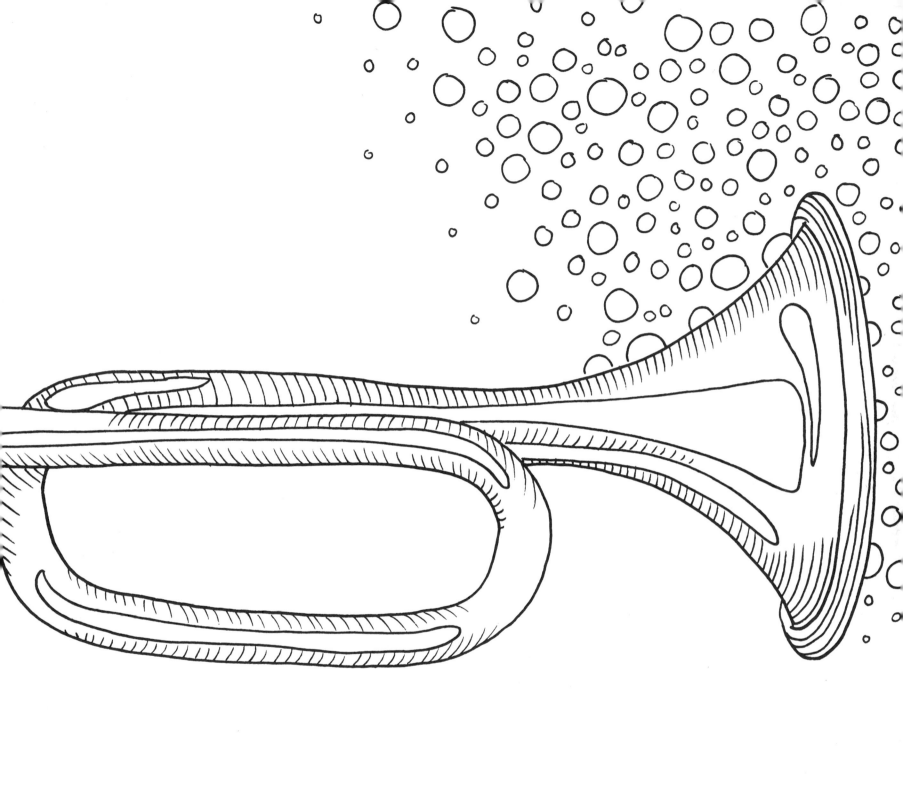

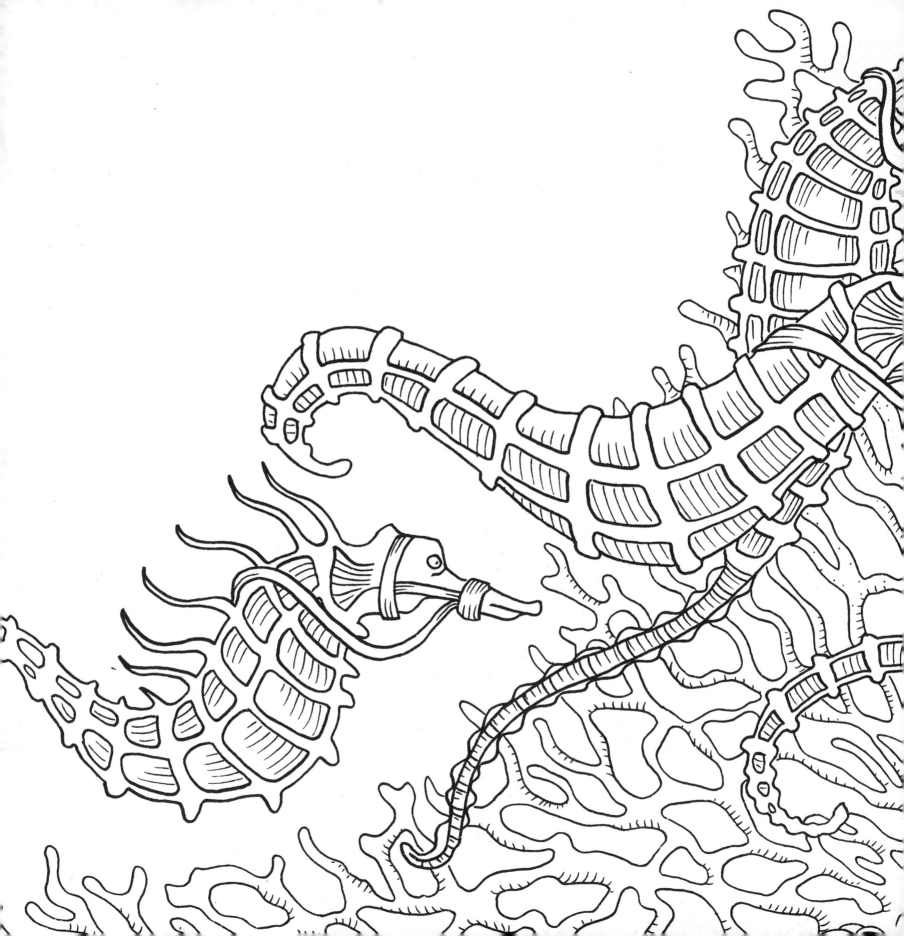

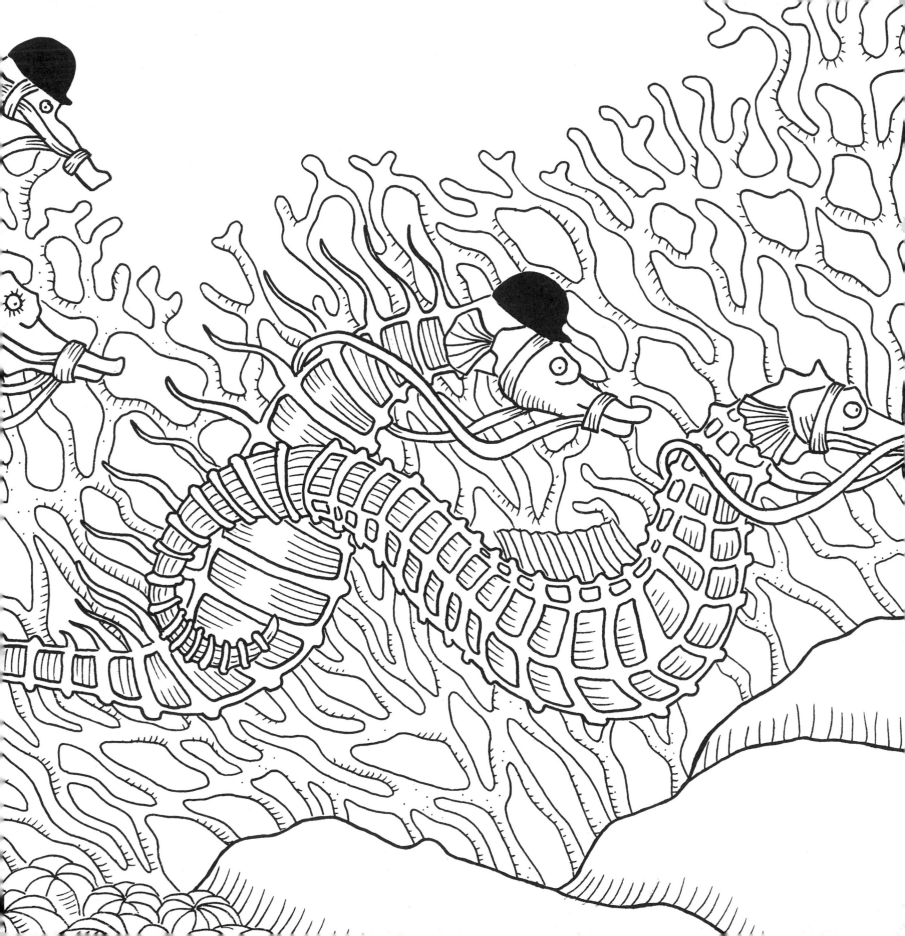

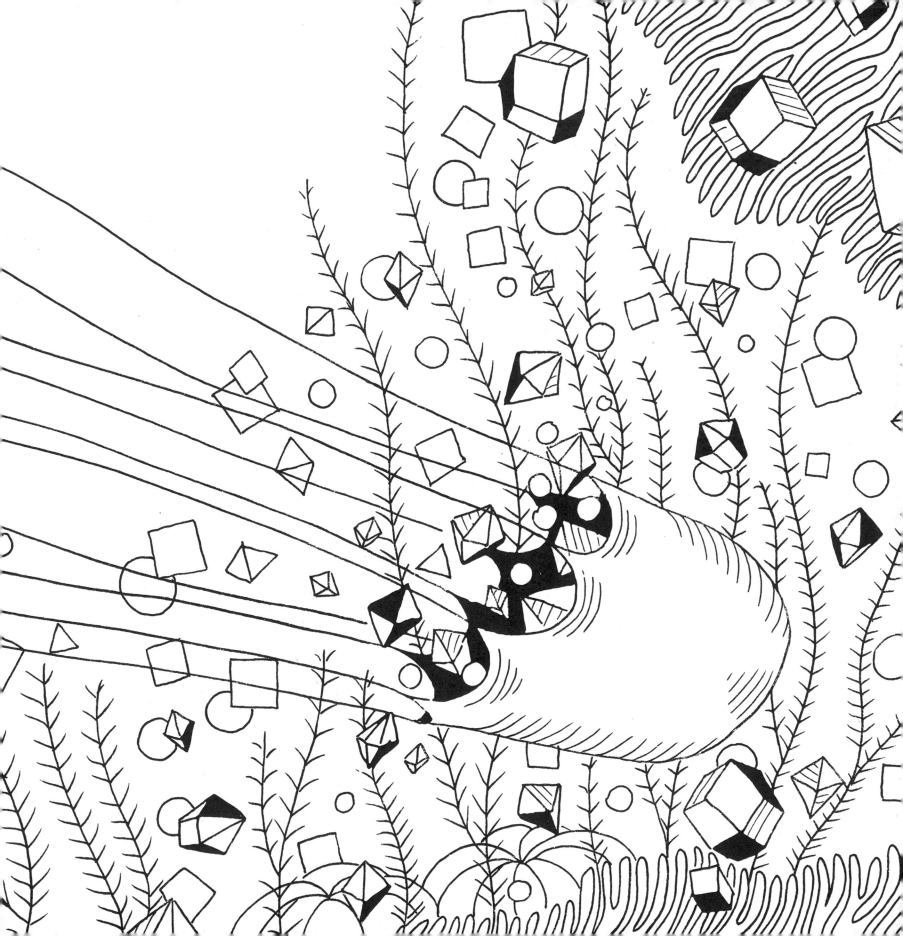

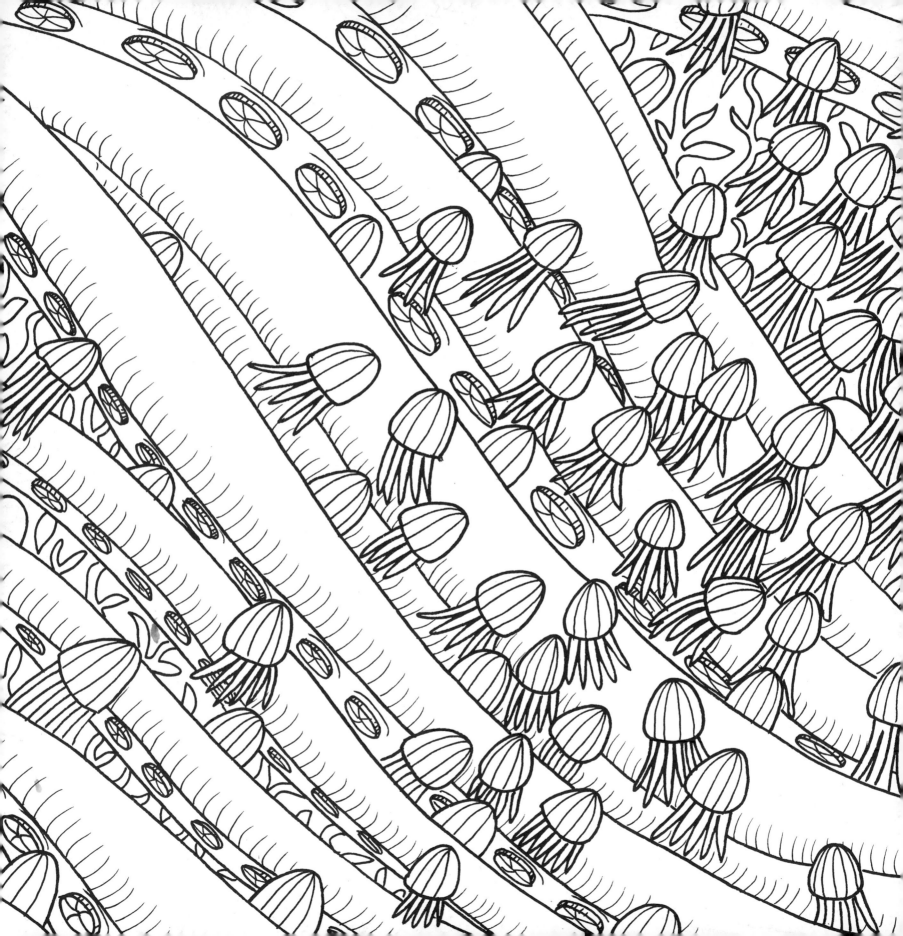

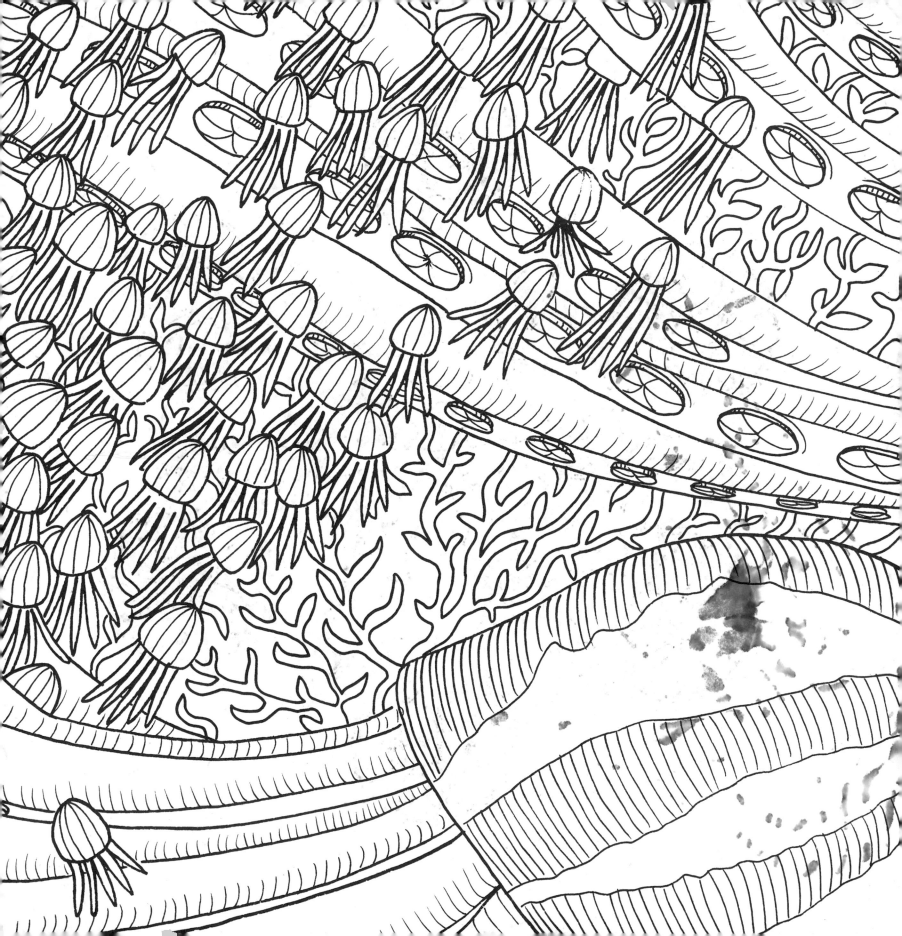

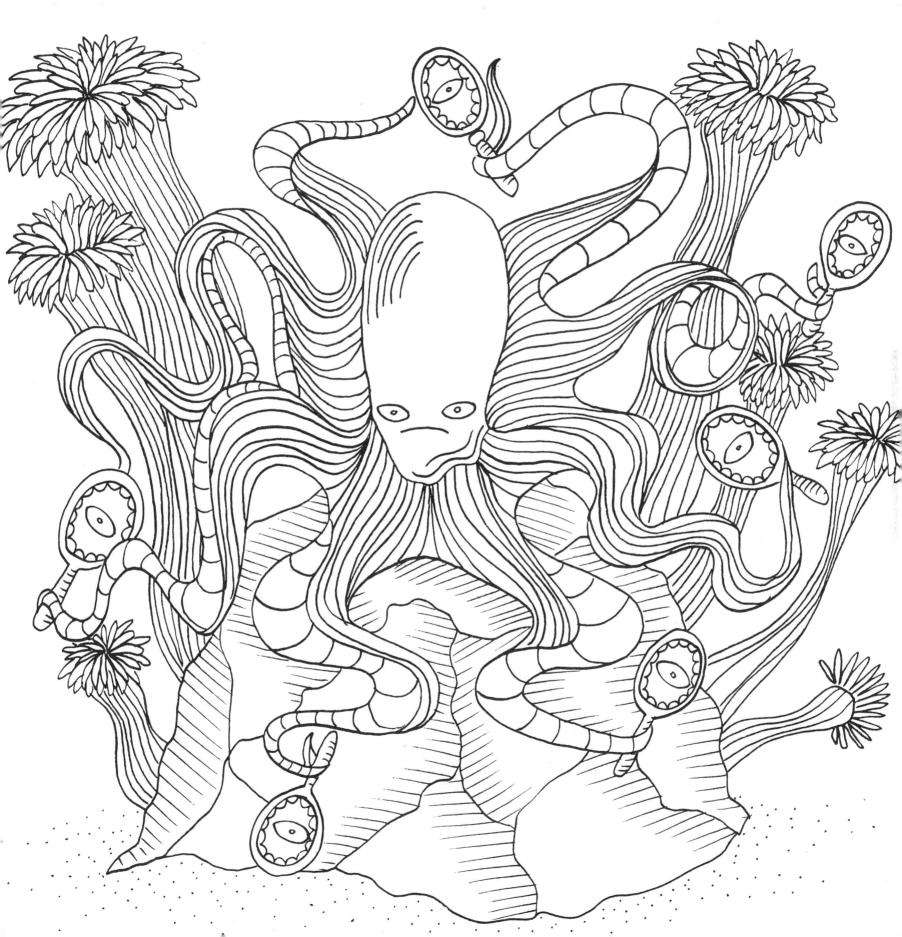

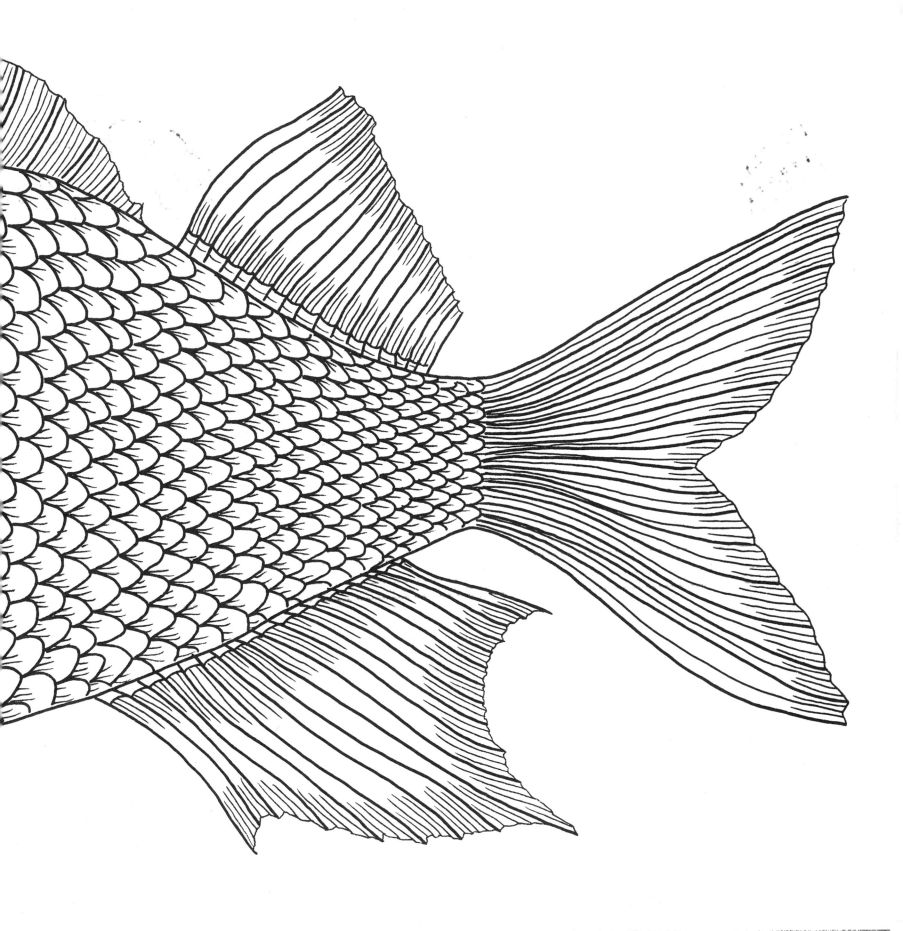

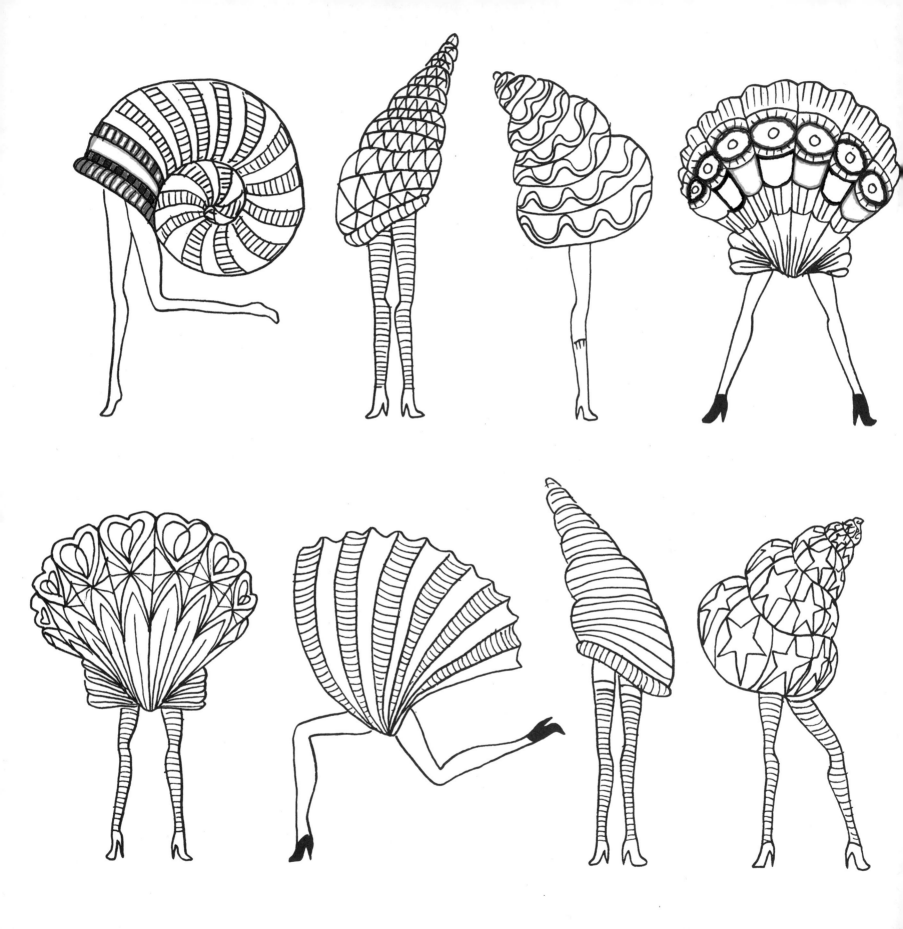

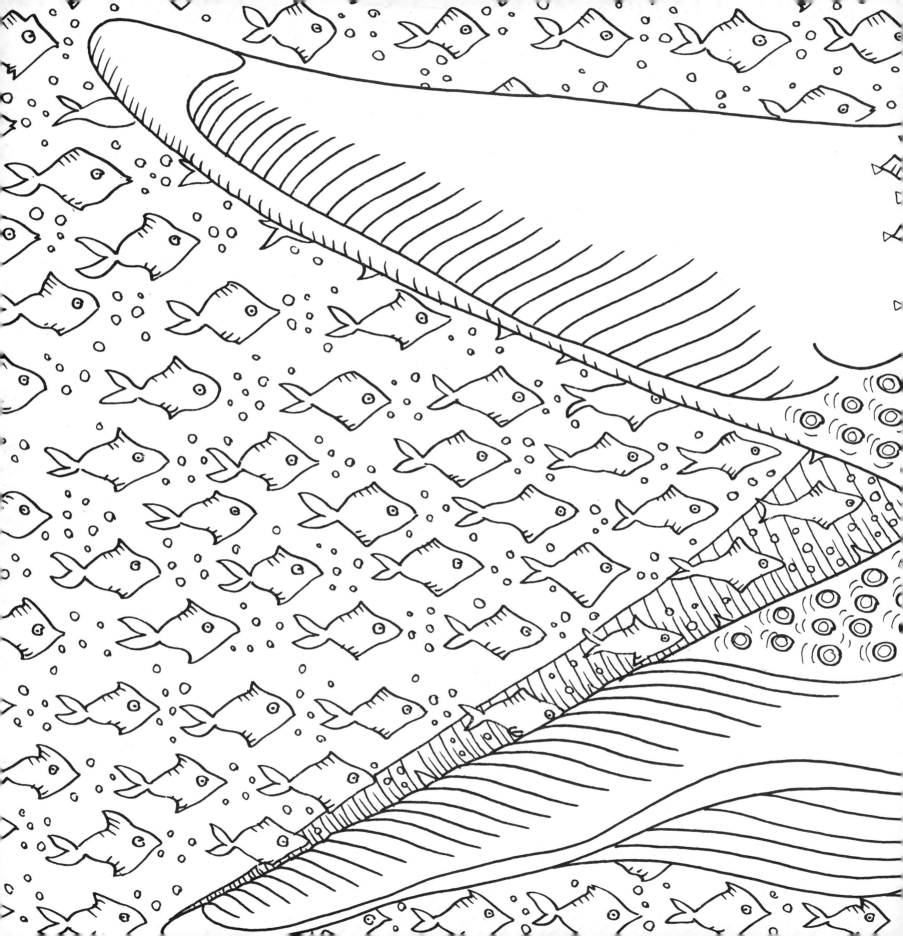

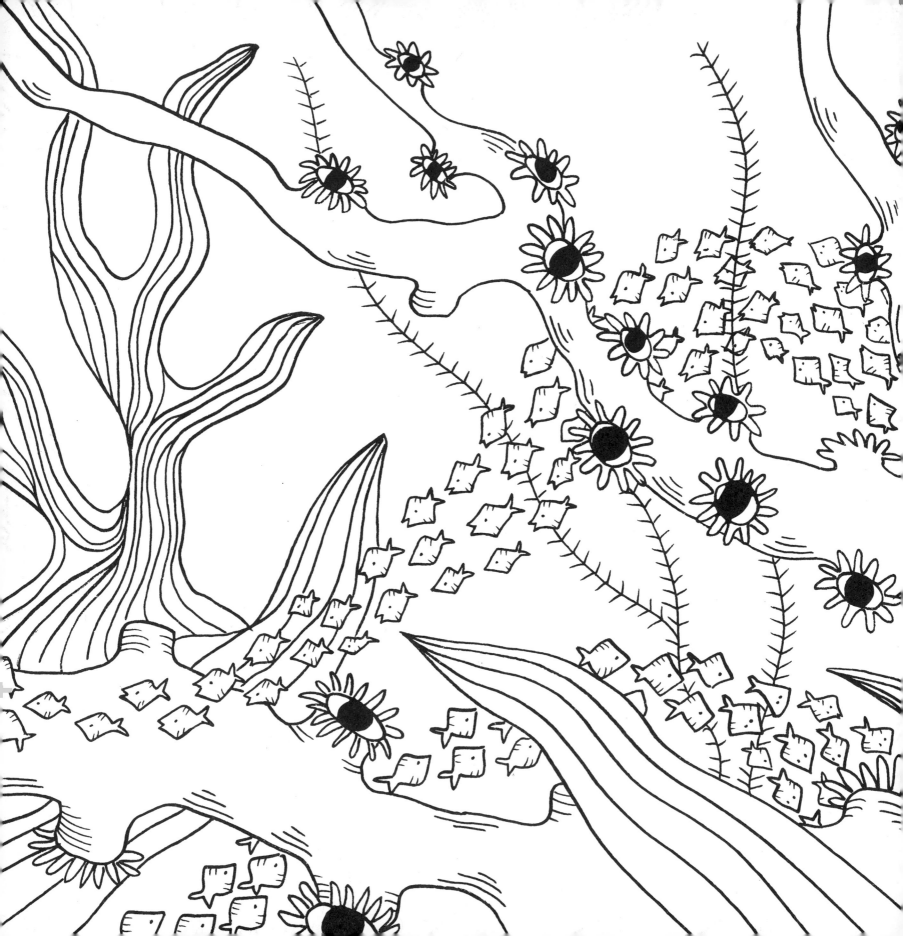

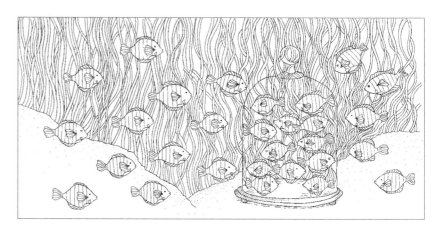
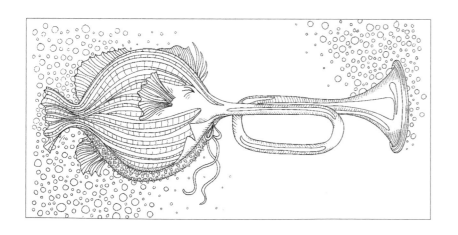

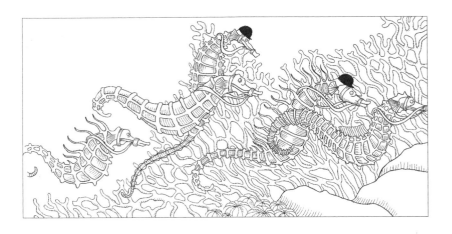

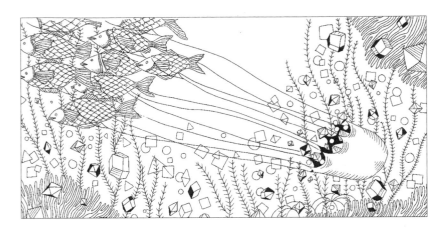

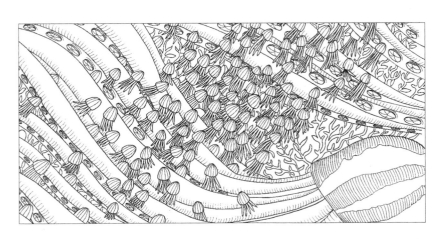

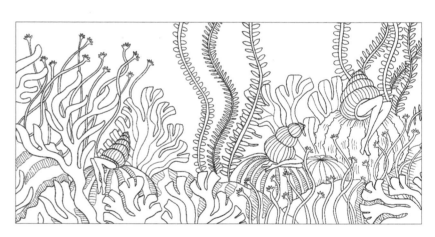

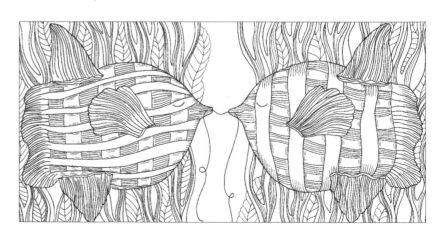

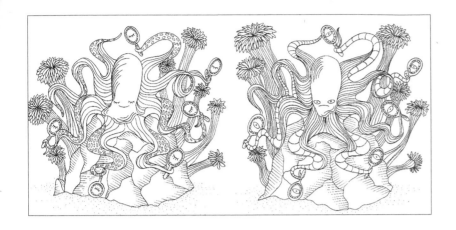
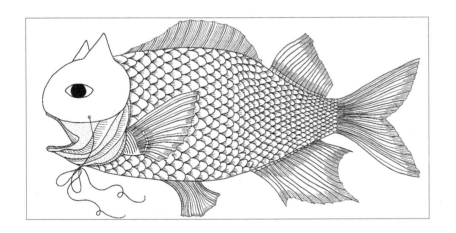
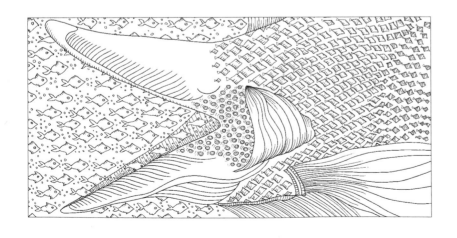

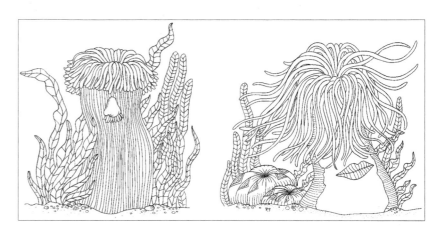

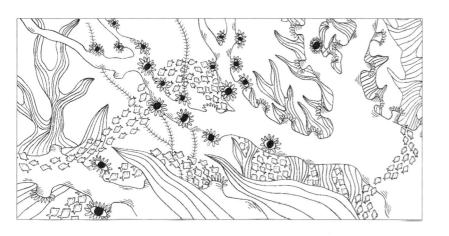

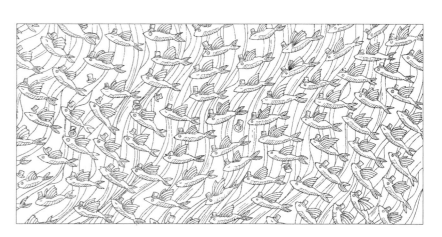

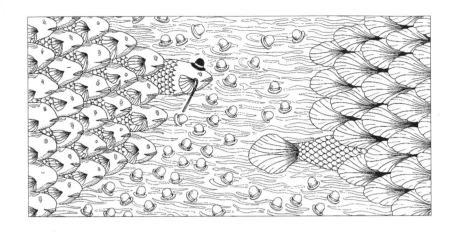

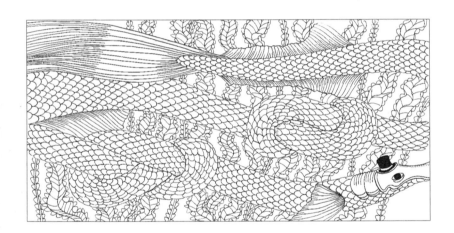